BETHLEHEM
ON THE LEHIGH

Ralph Grayson Schwarz

Bethlehem Area Foundation

Acknowledgements

The publication of this book has been made possible through the generosity of the Bethlehem Area Foundation in collaboration with the Bethlehem 250th Anniversary Committee.

Three repositories have been especially helpful in the production of this book: the Moravian Archives in Bethlehem, Pennsylvania (MAB), Vernon H. Nelson, Archivist; the Moravian Archives in Herrnhut, Germany (MAH), Ingeborg Baldauf, Archivist; and the Moravian Historical Society in Nazareth, Pennsylvania (MHS), Susan M. Dreydoppel, Executive Director.

Two individuals have contributed their extraordinary photographic talents to this book, Lee Butz and Hub Willson.

ISBN 0-9631444-1-3

Bethlehem Area Foundation
430 East Broad Street
Bethlehem, PA 18018

Printed and distributed by
Oaks Printing Company

Cover — View of Bethlehem, Pennsylvania, 1867 (Collection of Ralph Schwarz, Gustavus Grunewald, artist, 1867).

Contents

Foreword

Near the end of the eighteenth century, Moravian administrator Bishop John Ettwein prepared a plan for Bethlehem (p. 21). Envisioning eighty building lots, he observed, "The soil favors such a plan, the location makes it natural... Now everything is free and open for it!" His concerns for the future of Bethlehem were recorded just fifty years after the first buildings had been constructed on this virgin land. Ettwein never could have anticipated, that within again as many years, this community — first identified only by a large log Gemeinhaus called "house on the Lecha" — would be on the cutting edge of a new era. The Industrial Revolution would catalyze, reshape, and build Bethlehem on the Lehigh. Moravian initiative, doctrine, and missionary zeal would be reinforced and augmented with the participation and contribution of immigrating people blessed with cultures, skills, and attitudes which have expanded and energized this community. Bethlehem, approaching the twenty-first century, retains a unique balance between past, present, and future.

O Come All Ye Faithful

Count Nicolaus Ludwig von Zinzendorf, heir to one of Europe's leading families and spiritually influenced throughout his life by pietism, dedicated himself, his fortune, and his estate to Christian service. In 1722, he married Countess Erdmuth Dorothea von Reuss-Ebersdorf and purchased an estate at Berthelsdorf in Saxony (Germany) from his grandmother. That same year, he met Christian David and agreed to consider providing shelter for a group of oppressed Moravian refugees on his land. A settlement, not far from his Berthelsdorf manor house, was begun in December. By May, 1725, Christian David had journeyed to Moravia and Bohemia ten times to lead groups of settlers to the new town, named Herrnhut, meaning "under the Lord's watch." Descendants of the Hussites, these people were destined to become the core of the renewed Moravian Church and to take the gospel of Christ, for which they had suffered so long and so intensely, to peoples on five continents in the next few decades — beginning in 1732. On August 21, 1732, the birthday of Moravian missions, two men set out from Herrnhut, Leonard Dober and David Nitschmann (later, Bishop and founder of Bethlehem, Pennsylvania). After almost ten weeks at sea, they arrived at St. Thomas in the Danish West Indies on December 13, 1732. Nitschmann remained until April, long enough to help Dober establish himself.

A colony of Schwenkfelders, exiles from Silesia, had come to Herrnhut in 1725 under Count Zinzendorf's protection. By a royal edict of 1733 they were required to leave Saxony, and a small group went to Pennsylvania that year. A second and larger colony arrived in Philadelphia on September 22, 1734. They were conducted by George Boehnisch, one of the Moravian brethren; Christopher Baus, a Hungarian of Goerlitz, who had joined the Moravian brethren; and Christopher Wiegner, a Silesian, who had entered into close association with the brethren. Boehnisch remained three years until the fall of 1737 when he returned to Europe. During that period he helped Wiegner build his house and open his farm in the Skippack woods (present-day Montgomery County).

At the same time, Henry Antes, who had immigrated from the Palatinate to the Philadelphia area with his father and mother in 1720 and had married in 1726, purchased 200 acres of land in Frederick Township in 1735 (present-day Montgomery County), where he completed his grist mill and house in 1736. He had become one of the most influential, respected, and godly Germans in Pennsylvania.

Christopher Wiegner and George Boehnisch, as lay-evangelists among adults and children on the spiritually destitute frontier, brought together a circle of earnest men of various creeds and persuasions for the propagation of piety regardless of sectarian lines — a non-denominational union, "The Associated Brethren of Skippack." Henry Antes became its leading spirit. The Wiegner and Antes homesteads were centers of evangelical activity and were yet to become, in modern parlance, staging areas for Moravian migration and ultimate settlement in Nazareth and Bethlehem.

Concurrently, August Gottlieb Spangenberg, a learned Lutheran who had joined the Moravians in 1733 at Herrnhut and who would ultimately become Zinzendorf's most valuable coadjutor and successor, brought a small group of Moravians to the new Province of Georgia to undertake missionary work among the Indians. They arrived at Savannah on March 22, 1735. A second colony of sixteen men and eight women followed them, arriving at Savannah on February 28, 1736 under the leadership of Bishop David Nitschmann. He had returned from St. Thomas in 1733 and had been ordained in Berlin as the first bishop of the renewed Moravian Church in March 1735. Nitschmann organized the Moravian colony in Georgia on a plan similar to Herrnhut and ordained Anton Seifert, installing him as pastor of the congregation. Spangenberg left for Pennsylvania in March and was followed by Nitschmann in April. In Pennsylvania, with Christopher Wiegner's home as a base, and, for the first time, in direct association with Henry Antes, they worked among the Schwenkfelders, gained much knowledge about the Indians from Conrad Weiser of Tulpehocken, and learned about the spiritual condition of the German population generally. In late June, Nitschmann left for Europe and Spangenberg visited St. Thomas, returning to Christopher Wiegner's house in November, 1736 by way of New York. It was on this return trip that he met Captain Nicholas Garrison of Staten Island who would ultimately render such valuable service to the church, transporting Moravian sea congregations to America.

Except for an interlude during the summer of 1737 requiring his presence in Savannah, Spangenberg remained at Wiegner's house laboring and learning, as before, until August 1739 when he returned to Europe. His period of preparation was at an end.

On October 15, 1738, Rev. Peter Boehler arrived at Savannah. He had become a Moravian in 1736 and was ordained a deacon in December, 1737. Like Spangenberg, he became a leading bishop of the Church, working as a theologian, preacher, evangelist and administrator during the next two decades. At Savannah, he found the Moravian colony in the process of dissolution. A number had left, others had died. Early in January, 1740, Rev. George Whitefield, the famous evangelist, arrived on his sloop at Savannah. When he sailed again, he took with him Peter Boehler and the remaining Moravian colonists as passengers to Philadelphia, arriving on April 25, 1740.

During the voyage from Savannah, Whitefield determined to establish "a Negro school in Pennsylvania where he proposed to take up land to settle a town..." On May 3, 1740, an agreement for the purchase of five thousand acres of land was made with William Allen of Philadelphia. Two days later when Whitefield and Boehler jointly conducted services at the houses of Wiegner and Antes, Whitefield proposed that Boehler superintend the building of the projected school and utilize the Moravians who were with him as a work force. Favorably disposed to accept the offer, Boehler, accompanied by Anton Seifert and Henry Antes, inspected the site. At Antes' house, on May 10, 1740, the contract was concluded. Boehler led the first group from Germantown to the new tract, which Whitefield named Nazareth, arriving on May 30, 1740 — the trip was made on foot in three days. In addition to Peter Boehler, the group was comprised of former Georgia colonists Johann Boehner, Martin Mack, Anton Siefert, David Zeisberger, Sr., Rosina Zeisberger, David Zeisberger, Jr., Johanna Hummel and the boys Benjamin Sommers and James. A log cabin was under roof by July, but the work proceeded slowly. Even with the temporary addition of workmen hired at other places, an excessively rainy season and other factors prevented the laying up of the foundation walls of the new building above the door sills by September. It was determined that there was no hope of completing the walls before

Count Nicolaus Ludwig von Zinzendorf, 1700-1760
(MAH, Johannes Kupetzky, artist, 1740).

Christian David 1691-1751 (MAH).

August Gottlieb Spangenberg, 1704-1792 (MAB, John Valentine Haidt, artist).

winter. A second house, of squared logs, was habitable by November. Boehler, learning that Whitefield had returned to Pennsylvania, went to Philadelphia in November. He found Whitefield greatly disturbed and was drawn into a major doctrinal encounter over the theory of predestination, resulting in Whitefield's decision to terminate Moravian involvement in the Nazareth project. Through the intervention of Nathanael Irish, they were permitted to remain in

the houses they had erected for the winter. Nathanael Irish had established a farm and mill at the mouth of the Saucon Creek on the Lehigh River (present-day Shimersville) prior to 1737. There he opened a land office as the agent of William Allen. Irish had learned to know Boehler during the summer. Boehler had frequently taken grain to the mill to be ground. Through several exchanges with Boehler, Irish offered to sell the Moravians a tract of 500 acres of William

Countess Erdmuth Dorothea von Reuss-Ebersdorf, 1700-1756, first wife of Count von Zinzendorf (MAH).

Anna Nitschmann, 1715-1760, second wife of Count von Zinzendorf (MAH).

Allen's land on the north bank of the Lehigh at the mouth of the Monocacy Creek, but no conclusion could be reached until word was received from Europe regarding plans for Moravian settlement in Pennsylvania.

Plans accelerated with the arrival of Bishop David Nitschmann in Philadelphia on December 5, 1740. Accompanying him from Europe were Father David Nitschmann, his uncle; Christian Froelich; Anna Nitschmann, daughter of Father Nitschmann and later the second wife of Count Zinzendorf; and Johanna Sophia Molther. They had come to put into action plans that had been taking shape in Europe which drew heavily upon Bishop Nitschmann's and Spangenberg's experiences in Pennsylvania. Anticipating preaching in the settlements, establishing schools for the hosts of neglected children and missions among the Indians, the plans were to be carried out from a central settlement. Bishop Nitschmann had been sent to Pennsylvania to found such a settlement. When Bishop Nitschmann and his party reached Nazareth, the selection of a site was given immediate attention. Nitschmann had brought word that Boehler was to return to Europe. Before his departure he introduced Nitschmann to Nathanael Irish who renewed his offer of the 500-acre tract at the mouth of the Monocacy Creek on the north bank of the Lehigh River.

Survey of 500-acre tract of land at the confluence of the Monocacy Creek and the Lehigh River for William Allen, October 9, 1736 (MAB).

Antes House, Frederick Township, Montgomery County, built in 1736 by Henry Antes, 1701-1755 (Timothy Noble, 1991).

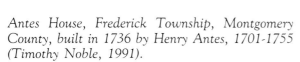

Bishop David Nitschmann, 1696-1772 (MAH).

8

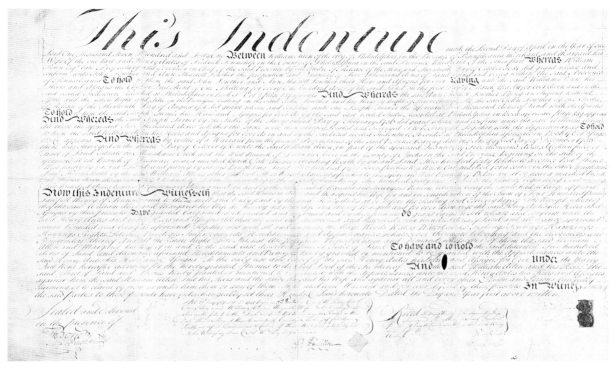

Deed for purchase of original 500-acre tract of land from William Allen and wife conveyed to Henry Antes, April 2, 1741. First real estate purchased by the Moravians in Pennsylvania (MAB).

Bishop Peter Boehler, 1712-1775 (MAB, John Valentine Haidt, artist).

Bishop Nathanael Seidel, 1718-1782 (MAB, John Valentine Haidt, artist).

Top left. Father David Nitschmann, 1676-1758 (MAB, John Valentine Haidt, artist).
Top right. Anton Seifert, 1712-1785 (Moravian College, John Valentine Haidt, artist).
Bottom left. John Martin Mack, 1715-1784 (MAB, John Valentine Haidt, artist).
Bottom right. George Neisser, 1715-1784 (MAB, John Valentine Haidt, artist).

With the exciting prospect of the land purchase in view, on December 22nd Father Nitschmann, Martin Mack and a third person, probably Anton Seifert or young David Zeisberger, went down to the "Allen tract" and felled the first tree at a spot selected by them. It was on the hillside along the Indian path that led up the hill from the spring near the Monocacy Creek ford (north of present-day Ohio Road and west of present-day Main Street behind the Hotel Bethlehem).

Bishop Nitschmann, who had departed with Boehler on December 27th, returned to the Moravian enclave on the Nazareth tract at the beginning of February, 1741. He had consulted with Antes about a number of alternative sites. Finally it was decided to let the lot decide the question and the result was in favor of closing with Nathanael Irish on the 500 acres.

On February 4th, they began to fell trees for a large house and for a small one to be assembled at the site they had selected in December. Bishop Nitschmann again enlisted the support of Henry Antes who had offered his help in every way possible. As there was neither a legal corporation or a naturalized citizen of the Province among the brethren, Antes executed the deed for the property in their behalf.

The two young women, Anna Nitschmann and Johanna Molther, who had arrived at the Naz-

View of Bethlehem, late spring 1749. Earliest general view of the community (MAB).

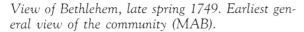
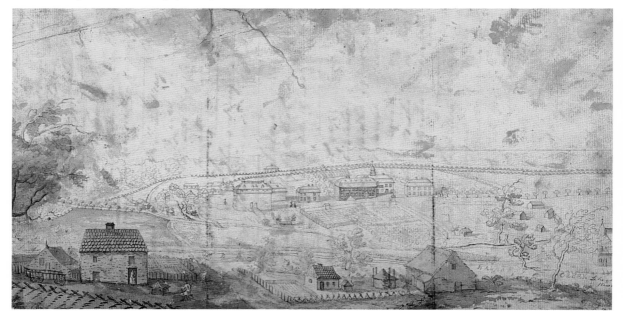

Nicholas Garrison, 1701-1781, captain of the "Irene" 1748-1755 (MAH).

Moravian ship, the snow "Irene". Moravian immigration to the British Colonies of North America dates from 1735. Four vessels, owned by the Moravian Church at different times, transported "sea congregations" for peopling the Moravian settlements. By 1762 more than six hundred men and women had been transported. The snow "Irene" was built by the Moravians at Staten Island, N.Y. During her service, between 1748 and 1757, she crossed the Atlantic twenty-four times, sailing between New York and ports in England and Holland and made one voyage to Greenland (MAH, Benjamin Garrison, artist).

areth tract with Bishop Nitschmann in December, left at the beginning of April to begin their tour of the settlements to prepare the way for extensive itinerant work. By June, the last of the pioneers on the Nazareth tract had removed to the new settlement on the Lehigh where they were preparing as much cleared land as possible for immediate cultivation. On June 28th they began squaring the timbers for the large house. George Neisser, who had been sent from Savannah to Christopher Wiegner's house in 1737, and remained under contract to Antes, rejoined the brethren at the new settlement.

While Bishop Nitschmann is the recognized founder of what was later to be named Bethlehem, the fourteen founding settlers of Bethlehem are Anton Seifert, David Zeisberger, Sr., Rosina Zeisberger, David Zeisberger, Jr., Martin Mack, Johanna Hummel, Benjamin Sommers, James, Johann Boehner, Matthias Seibold, Bishop David Nitschmann, Father David Nitschmann, Christian Froehlich, and George Neisser.

Zinzendorf's arrival in Pennsylvania in December, 1741 would not have been required simply to organize the new Moravian colony on the Lehigh. He had delegated that task to Bishop Nitschmann and Spangenberg. He had a larger

left. Elisabeth Boehler, nee Hopson, 1717-1781, wife of Bishop Peter Boehler (MAB, John Valentine Haidt, artist).
right. Anna Johanna Seidel, nee Piesch, 1726-1788, wife of Bishop Nathanael Seidel (MAH).

John Christopher Pyrlaeus, 1713-1785, began school in Gemeinhaus for teaching Indian languages to missionaries in 1744, David Zeisberger among them (MAH).

Count Zinzendorf and Conrad Weiser meet with heads and deputies of the Six Nations, Iroquois Confederacy, at Tulpehocken, August 3, 1742 (MAH).

David Zeisberger, 1721-1808, his illustrious missionary career among Indians lasted sixty years (MAB, John Valentine Haidt, artist).

John Gottlieb Ernst Heckewelder, 1743-1823, missionary and expert in Indian languages and traditions (American Philosophical Society, John Lewis Krimmel, artist, 1820).

Baptism of Indians in 1751 Chapel (MAB).

left. Michael, a Monsey Indian, Moravian Indian from Shekomeko. After massacre at Gnadenhuetten, he came to live in Brethren's House at Bethlehem where he died in 1758 (MAB, Rufus A. Grider).

left. Bishop John Christopher Frederick Cammerhoff, 1721-1751 (MAB, John Valentine Haidt, artist).
right. Frederick Martin, 1704-1750 (MAH).

left. Gottlieb Pezold, 1720-1762 (MAB, John Valentine Haidt, artist).
right. Bernhard Adam Grube, 1715-1808 (MHS).

left. John Jacob Schmick, 1714-1778 (MHS, John Valentine Haidt, artist).
right. Johanna Schmick nee Ingerheidt, 1721-1795 (MHS, John Valentine Haidt, artist).

13

above, Vignette and p. 15, View. Bethlehem Tract with all the adjacent Land, 1755 (MHS, Andreas Hoeger, delineator, 1755).

purpose in mind for Pennsylvania — a "Congregation of God in the Spirit". His ecumenical vision was, regrettably, ahead of his time. His first meeting with Antes proved central to his objective. Within a few days Antes issued a circular calling for a Conference of Religions.

Arriving at the new settlement of the brethren on the Lehigh on December 21st, Zinzendorf and his party occupied two rooms on the second floor of the western end of the as yet unfinished Gemeinhaus. At a Christmas Eve vigil in the first house, Zinzendorf named the settlement Bethlehem. His party left Bethlehem Christmas morning, engaging in a rigorous schedule of preaching, publishing, and participating in seven Conferences of Religions during the next six months,

primarily in Philadelphia and Germantown.

The first sea congregation, consisting of fifty-seven persons including George Piesch, who was the general conductor, and Peter Boehler, who was chaplain, left London March 16, 1742 and finally arrived in Philadelphia by way of New York on June 7th. They were greeted upon their June 21st arrival in Bethlehem by Zinzendorf, who had preceded them. The first organization of the people for communal life began on the 24th when the eighty people present were divided into two groups. One was called the itinerent or pilgrim congregation, and the other, the home or local congregation. This initial framework set a pattern for organizational structure in Bethlehem during the following two decades.

Zinzendorf's first tour among the Delaware Indians included an unplanned stop at Conrad Weiser's house in Tulpehocken on August 3rd.

He had gotten to know Weiser through the Conferences of Religions (Pennsylvania Synods). There he met the deputies of the Six Nations (Iroquois Confederacy) who were returning from a conference with Governor Thomas in Philadelphia. Zinzendorf's visit with the Indians resulted in a pact of friendship giving the brethren permission to travel freely among the Six Nations. Zinzendorf left Bethlehem for his return to Europe on December 31, 1742.

Peter Boehler had returned with the first sea congregation to Bethlehem where he remained active until he returned to Europe in 1745. He was consecrated a bishop in London in 1748 and was again active in Bethlehem between 1753 and 1764.

The first sea congregation also brought Nathanael Seidel to Bethlehem in 1742. A missionary among the Indians and white settlers, he made many journeys, always on foot. He was consecrated a bishop in Herrnhut in 1758. After Zinzendorf's death, necessitating Spangenberg's return to Europe, Seidel assumed general superintendence of Moravian work in America until his death in Bethlehem in 1782.

Bishop Nitschmann returned to Bethlehem in the fall of 1742 and had general charge of Indian affairs until November 1744. He was in Bethlehem again in 1748 and led a large sea congregation to Bethlehem in 1755.

August Gottlieb Spangenberg was ordained a bishop in June, 1744. He was administrator in Bethlehem from November 1744 through 1748. He returned in 1751 and 1753. His final sojourn in Bethlehem occurred between April 22, 1754 and June 22, 1762 when he returned to Europe to assume primary leadership following the death of Zinzendorf in 1760.

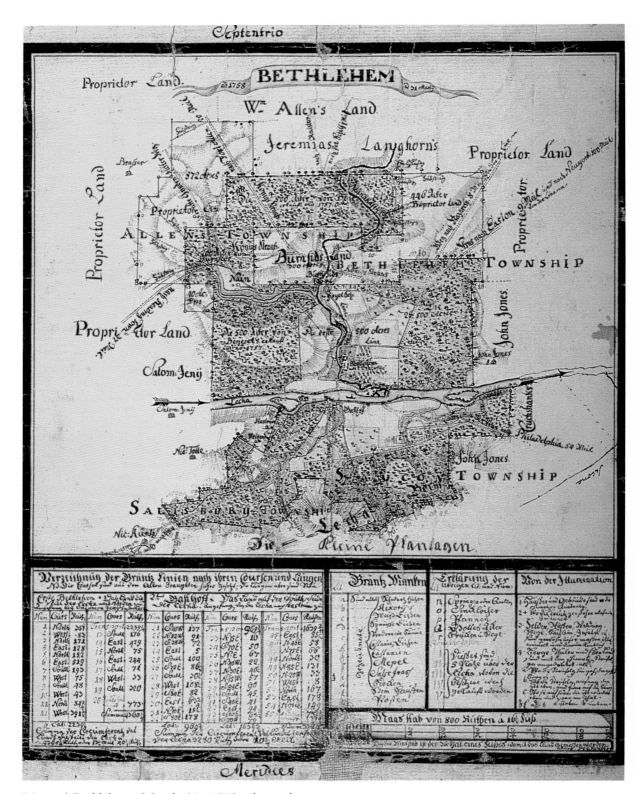

Map of Bethlehem, March 31, 1758, shows first
500 acres and Burnsides Plantation (MAB, Philipp
Reuter, delineator, 1758).

Transition to a Private Economy

Moravian missionary efforts in America were severely reduced after Count Zinzendorf died in the spring of 1760. The leaders of the church in Herrnhut made a settlement with the Zinzendorf family and assumed the huge debts that the Count had incurred on behalf of the Moravian Church. Bethlehem accepted its pro-rated share of the debt and received, in return, ownership of its own 4,000 acres of land, its buildings, and mills. The transition of Bethlehem from a "general economy" to a private economy had begun. Ownership of the land gave the leaders of the Bethlehem community more than economic power. They used their control of the land to maintain a village exclusively made up of Moravians. All aspects of commercial activity were closely regulated by a Board of Supervisors. At first the congregation leaders kept control of the farms, the inns, the store, and the apothecary, as well as most of the industrial quarter including various mills, the tannery, blacksmith shop, and pottery. As the privatization of the economy evolved, a lease system was established. People could own the buildings in which they lived and worked but they were required to lease the land on which the buildings stood.

The privatization of the Bethlehem economy had a significant effect on the village landscape. Private dwelling houses and gardens were added. Some of the institutional buildings were converted for family use, while others were expanded for their traditional uses. The farm yard, still in its original location in 1766 (p. 18), was largely relocated by 1771 (p. 19). The following year a new horse barn was built south of the Sun Inn and the relocation was completed. The town plans together with the Garrison view (p. 20) depict the village during the stressful conditions which affected the community during the American revolution.

John Ettwein was the administrator in Bethlehem during the revolution and for several decades thereafter. He provided courageous leadership during the period of 1776-1778, when set-backs suffered by Washington's continental forces had a direct involvement on Bethlehem. The General Hospital of the army occupied the Single Brethren's House from December 1776 to March 1777 and again from September 1777 to June 1778. Important statesmen and hundreds of soldiers were present in the heavily burdened but supportive community.

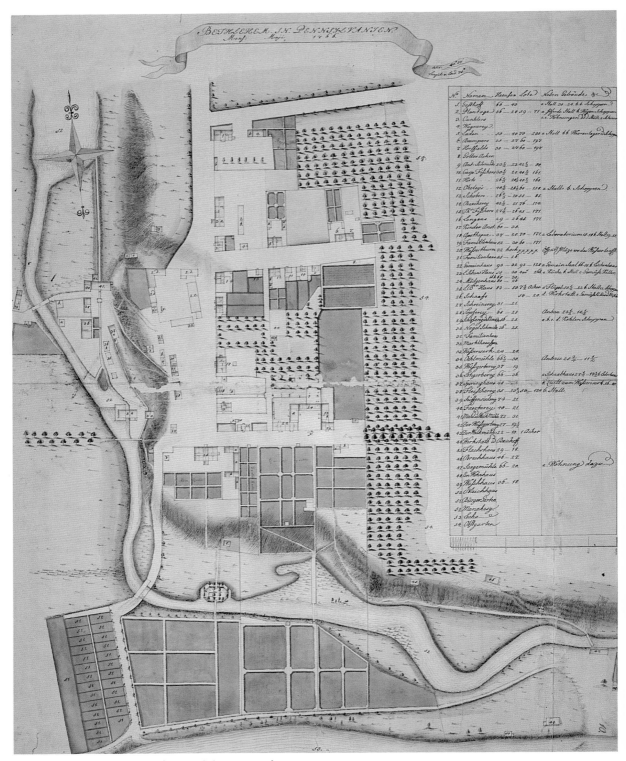

Plan of Bethlehem in Pennsylvania, May 1766, shows
first floor plan of every building (MAH).

Bethlehem in Pennsylvania
May 1766

1. *Sun Inn*
2. *Farm*
3. *Daniel and Maria Kunckler House*
4. *Wheelwright*
5. *Store*
6. *Abraham and Rachel Boemper House*
7. *Timothy and Mary Horsfield House*
8. *God's Acre*
9. *Anton and Beata Schmidt House*
10. *Caspar and Christina Fischer House*
11. *Johann Tobias and Maria Hirte House*
12. *John and Elizabeth Okeley House*
13. *Andreas and Hedwig Regina Schober House*
14. *Bakery*
15. *Thomas and Agnes Fischer House*
16. *Gottlieb and Margaretha Catharina Lange House*
17. *Children's School*
18. *Apothecary*
19. *Married Couples' House*
20. *Water Tower*
21. *Married Couples' House*
22. *Gemeinhaus*
23. *Single Sisters' House*
24. *Girls' Seminary House*
25. *Single Brethren's House*
26. *Thomas Schaaf House*
27. *Carpenter Shop*
28. *Pottery*
29. *Locksmith and Blacksmith (Forge)*
30. *Nail Smith*
31. *Married Couples' House*
32. *Little Market House*
33. *Water Works*
34. *Oil Mill*
35. *Tannery (White Leather)*
36. *Tannery*
37. *Spring House*
38. *Slaughter House (Butcher Shop)*
39. *Soapmaking House*
40. *Dyehouse*
41. *Flour and Fulling Mill*
42. *Belonging to the Tannery (White)*
43. *Belonging to the Fulling Mill*
44. *Workshop and Building Yard*
45. *Flax House*
46. *Breakhouse*
47. *Sawmill*
48. *A Dwelling House*
49. *Washhouse*
50. *Bleach House*
51. *Citizens' Gardens*
52. *Monocacy Creek*
53. *Lehigh River*
54. *Orchard*

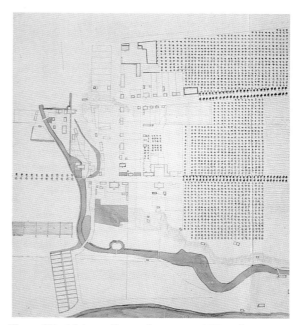

Plan of Bethlehem, Pennsylvania, c. 1771, shows most of original farm buildings relocated from west side to east side of Main Street (MAH).

Detail of View of Bethlehem, 1784, shows relocated farm buildings on east side of Main Street (MAB, Nicholas Garrison, Jr., artist, 1784).

Bishop John Ettwein, 1721-1802, administrator of Bethlehem during the American Revolution (MHS, John Valentine Haidt, artist, c. 1754).

Joannetta Maria Ettwein, nee Kymbel, 1725-1789, wife of Bishop Ettwein (MHS, John Valentine Haidt, artist, c. 1754).

View of Bethlehem from the north, c. 1780, shows how the village looked during the period of the American Revolution (MAB, Nicholas Garrison, Jr., artist, c. 1780).

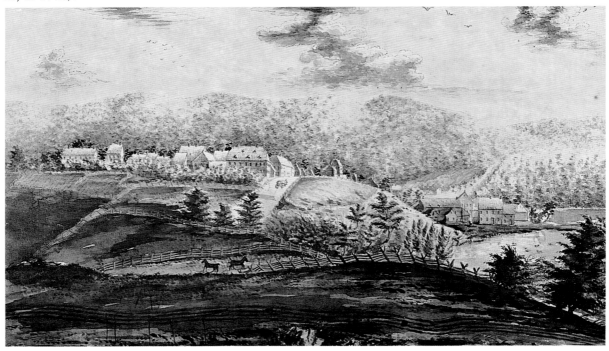

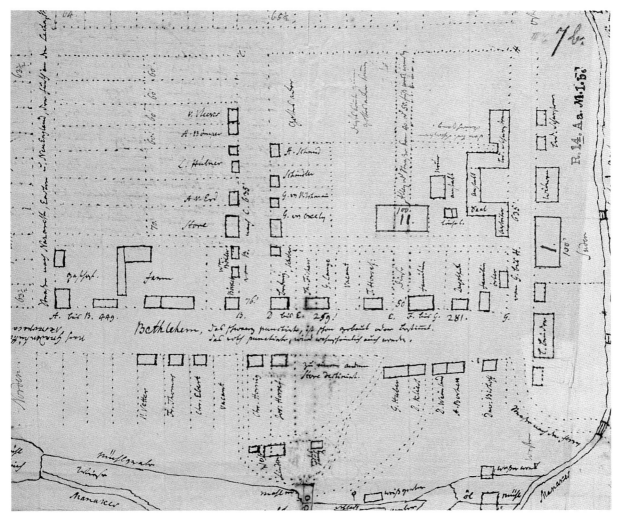

Plan of Bethlehem, February 16, 1791, memorandum signed by John Ettwein. "I do not say that Bethlehem will become like this: But I can still say that it **can** become like this: Herrnhut has 100 building sites, this plan already contains 80: Why should one consider it foolish, if one says: in 20, 30, 40 years, all these lots will be resided on, when the plan has so approved of it.

The soil favors such a plan, the location makes it natural. Some towns are lying higher and yet have water. The precaution should however be taken, that no immovable obstructions are made against such a plan. Now everything is still free and open for it!" (MAH, John Ettwein, delineator, 1791).

In 1791, the physical requirements of the community were addressed by Bishop Ettwein. Anticipating the construction of what would become Central Church, he proposed alternative sites and laid out additional building lots. Residential and commercial expansion in the 1780's initiated the development of Main Street north to the Sun Inn. The townscape was changing from that of an informal village on a hillside to one with a street grid. The first bridge across the Lehigh River was constructed in 1794, significantly altering the approach to the town.

Detail of View of Bethlehem, 1793, last view before the building of the first bridge across the Lehigh (MAB, George Fetter, artist, 1793).

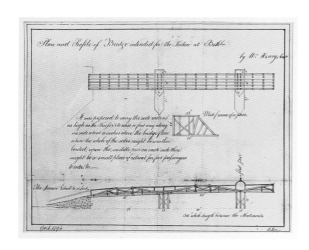

Plan and Profile of Bridge intended for the Lehigh at Bethlehem, October 4, 1794 (Kemerer Museum of Decorative Arts, W. Henry, delineator, 1794).

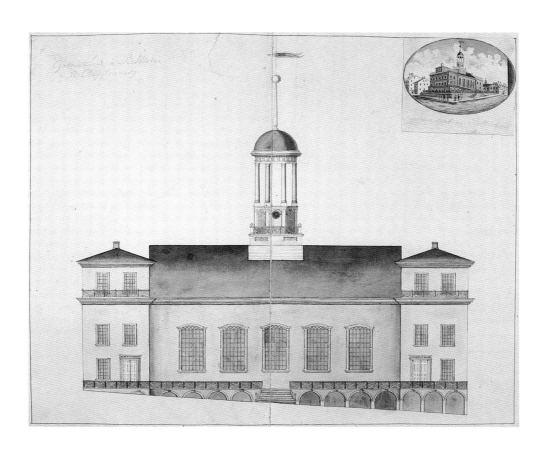

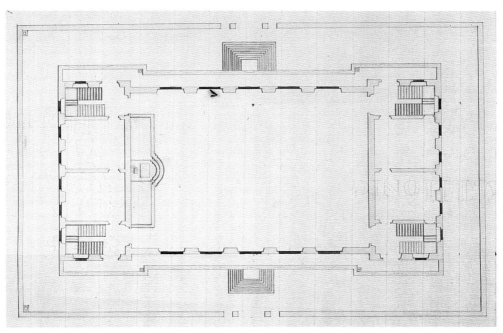

Elevation and plan of Central Church, presumably as built (MAH, c. 1806).

Draught of the Land at Bethlehem, December 31, 1812 (MAB, F.C. Kampman, delineator, 1812).

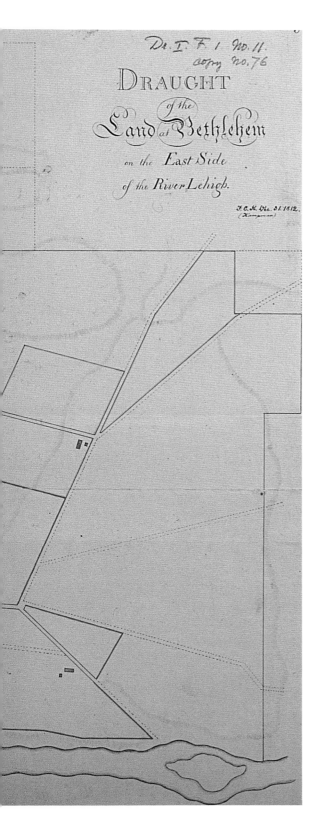

Dr. I.F. / no. 11.
copy no. 76

DRAUGHT
of the
Land *at* Bethlehem
on the East Side
of the River Lehigh.

F.C.K. Dic. 31. 1812.
(*Xempener*)

Gradual Change to the Creation of Secular Government

With the completion of the first bridge in 1794 and Central Church in 1806, the Bethlehem landscape was altered in a significant way. Visitors to Bethlehem during the early nineteenth-century wrote and published their observations. They were impressed by the size and beauty of the church, with the quality of services at the Sun Inn, with the quality of craftsmen's products sold at reasonable prices, and by the mechanical complexities of the mills and the water distribution system.

In 1812, agitation created by the owners of shops, stores, and residences on Main Street resulted in the relocation of the old farm which had been totally moved to the east side of Main Street after 1772. The farm buildings were remodelled for residential and commercial use and new farm buildings were erected east of the village, just south of present-day Market Street and east of present-day High Street.

Adjustments after the abandonment of the "general economy" and restrictive regime administered from Europe resulted in a population decline. The population was inflated to 800 during the Indian uprisings in 1756-57 due to refugees. The actual high in 1761 was 659. It declined to 470 permanent residents in 1818.

The relaxation of restrictions on some economic activities came as an accomodation to the pressures of two decades of increased prosperity and raised expectations throughout the Lehigh Valley.

Canal development had gripped the nation and the community. Construction of the Lehigh Canal reached Bethlehem in 1827 and it was open for traffic in June 1829 under a state charter granted to the Lehigh Coal and Navigation Company. The canal linked Bethlehem economically to the region and the nation. The congregation voted to abolish the lease system in January, 1844, and final incorporation of the Borough of Bethlehem came a year later.

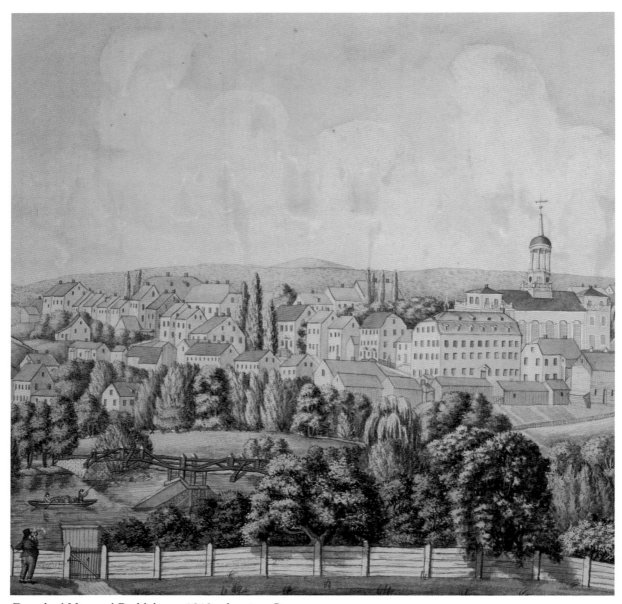

Detail of View of Bethlehem, 1812, showing Central Church completed in 1806 and the bridge completed in 1794 (MAB, probably Samuel Reinke, artist, 1812).

View of the east side of Main Street north of Market Street, shows 1757 horse stable as converted to apartments in 1812 (MAB, Rufus A. Grider, artist, 1840).

View of the east side of Main Street north of Market Street, shows how grading of Main Street exposed basement levels at new grade providing commercial space (MAB, Rufus A. Grider, artist, 1850).

View of the Lehigh River and Canal from Mt. Rogers look-
ing east, July 14, 1851 (MAB, Rufus A. Grider, artist, 1851).

View of lock on the Lehigh Canal (Kemerer Museum of Decorative Arts, Gustavus Grunewald, artist, 1834).

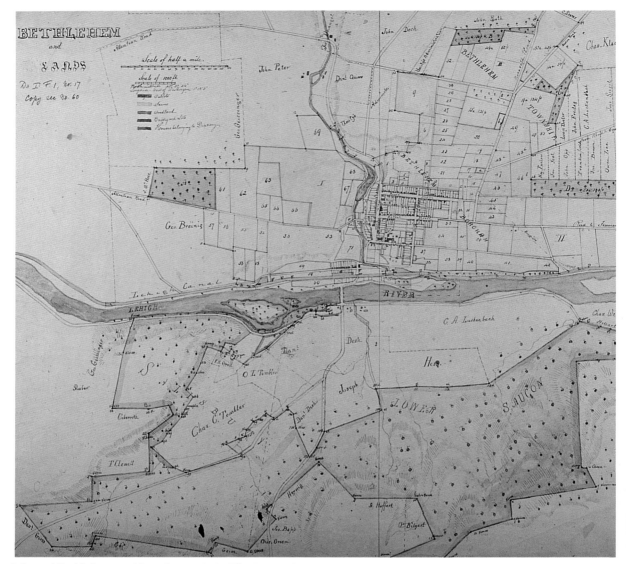

Map of Bethlehem and Lands, c. 1848. The Borough of Bethlehem, incorporated March 6, 1845 is shown here. The population at the close of 1845, including about 150 non-Moravians who lived within the Borough, was about 1,050 (MAB).

Map of Bethlehem and the New Town of Wetherill, Northampton County, Pa., 1855. The Lehigh Valley Railroad completed its line between Mauch Chunk and Easton in 1855 and selected South Bethlehem as its headquarters (MAB, W.Th. Roepper, Surveyor and delineator, 1855).

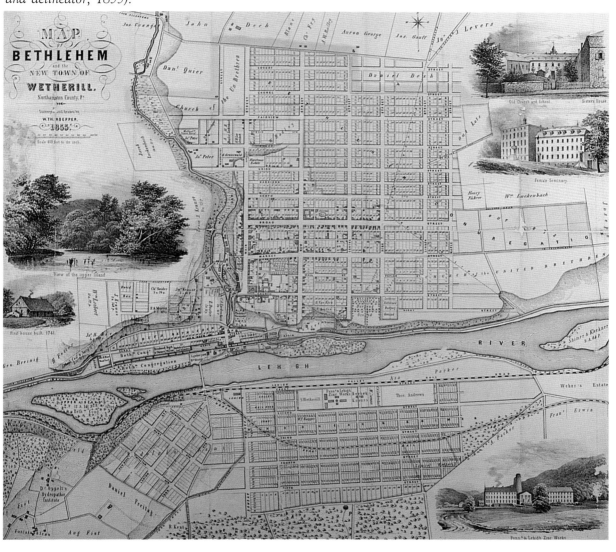

pp. 34-35 View of Bethlehem from the north, c. 1855 (MAB, Gustavus Grunewald, artist, c. 1855).

Asa Packer, 1805-1879, President of the Lehigh Valley Railroad.

(Lehigh University, DeWitt Clinton Boutelle, artist, 1873).

At the Cutting Edge of the Industrial Revolution

Robert Heysham Sayre, 1824-1907, Chief Engineer and General Superintendent of the Lehigh Valley Railroad (Lehigh University, DeWitt Clinton Boutelle, artist).

The decision of the Moravian congregation to abolish the lease system in January, 1844 heralded a new era of development. In 1847, Charles Augustus Luckenbach purchased 1,380 acres of the congregation's farm lands, including four farms that made up south Bethlehem and Fountain Hill. This acreage was for the most part resold and divided into residential and industrial sites. The rapid growth of what was to become the Borough of South Bethlehem accelerated with the opening of the Lehigh Valley Railroad in 1855 and its convergence with the North Penn Railroad after 1857.

One name stands pre-eminent in the development of the Lehigh Valley Railroad — Asa Packer. The construction of Asa Packer's railroad was, however, largely a testament to the engineering and operational skills of Robert H. Sayre. South Bethlehem became the focal point of the railroad company's operations, with direct connections to New York and Philadelphia.

The growth of the iron producing industry in the Lehigh Valley area stimulated the opening of new ore mines. In the early 1850's substantial deposits of workable iron ore were discovered in the Saucon Valley area south of Bethlehem. In 1857, a group of Bethlehem citizens led by Augustus Wolle, a wealthy Moravian merchant, organized the Saucona Iron Company to exploit these newly discovered deposits. In 1860, before the ground was broken for the first furnace, strategically located along the tracks of the Lehigh Valley Railroad in south Bethlehem, the company's name was changed to Bethlehem Rolling Mills & Iron Company. Asa Packer was a prime backer of the new company.

Lehigh University, 1894, Asa Packer, Founder, 1865 (MAB).

John Fritz, 1822-1913, Ironmaster (Lehigh University, Paul Hercher, artist, 1898).

Perhaps the single most important factor in determining the infant company's success was obtaining the services of John Fritz. Robert Sayre, chief engineer of the Lehigh Valley Railroad, was instrumental in attracting the talented John Fritz to run the newly renamed and recapitalized Bethlehem Iron Company works. The coming of the Civil War slowed development of a plant to roll iron rails. Finally, in 1863 John Fritz put the first furnace in blast. A second furnace started production of iron in 1867 and a third in 1868.

The Bethlehem Iron Company became the Lehigh Valley's first steel producer when the first steel rails were rolled at the new Bessemer Works in 1873. Plans were developed by the company in 1885 for the establishment of a complete forge plant. The company became the first plant in the United States to make steel armor plate and forgings for military cannon. During the next twenty years the output of the new Ordinance, *(Ordnance)* Forging Plant and Armor Plate Department became the major part of the company's business. Under John Fritz's able management the firm continued to grow and prosper.

As industry grew along the banks of the Lehigh River, South Bethlehem swelled with immigrants and residents of outlying rural communities who came to work in its many plants and shops.

The Irish, Germans and Pennsylvania-Germans were the primary groups to settle during the 1860's and 1870's. In 1865 the Borough of South Bethlehem was officially organized. The Irish comprised a third of the town by 1880. Slovaks began coming in 1878, followed by Hungarians. Ukranians and Poles started arriving in the late 1880's. Many Slovenes, also called Windish, began arriving in the early 1890's. The first Italians came in 1895. Around the turn of the century, immigrants came from Russia, Greece, Lithuania, and Croatia. Mexicans arrived following World War I and the first Puerto Ricans began to arrive during the 1930's, increasing substantially during World War II.

Each ethnic group coming to the borough established its own nationality-affiliated churches and social organizations. In a development common to other American cities, as each new wave of immigrants arrived, it would take the place of the immediate predecessors at the bottom of the social scale.

pp. 40-41 View of Bethlehem, Pennsylvania, 1867. Possibly one of the last paintings by Gustavus Grunewald, 1805-1878, before his final departure from Bethlehem to Europe, mid-July 1867 (Collection of Ralph Schwarz, Gustavus Grunewald, artist, 1867).

pp. 42-43 Birds-Eye View of the Bethlehems, Pa., 1873 (MAB, O.H. Bailey, delineator, Strobridge & Co. Lithographer, 1873).

pp. 44-45 The Boroughs of Bethlehem, South, and West Bethlehem, Pennsylvania, 1886 (MAB, O.H. Bailey, delineator, O.H. Bailey & Co. Lithographer, 1886).

pp. 46-47 West Bethlehem, Lehigh County, Pennsylvania, 1894 (MAB, T.M. Fowler, delineator, T.M. Fowler & James B. Moyer, Publisher, 1894).

pp. 48-49 Bessemer Converter, Bethlehem Iron Co. Plant, 1895 (Bethlehem Steel, S.B. Shiley, artist, 1895).

Bethlehem References.

1. Moravian College.
2. " Boarding School.
3. " Day School.
4. " Church.
5. High School.
6. Public Schools.
7. Citizens Hall.
8. Eagle Hotel.
9. American House.
10. Fetters Hotel.
11. L. & S. Depot.
12. Bethlehem Mills.
13. Moravian Chair Factory.
14. J. A. Wildrick's Church and Parlor Organ Manufactory.

CHURCHES.

15. Moravian.
16. Methodist.
17. " German.
18. Lutheran.
19. " German.
20. Reformed.
21. Episcopal.
22. United Brethren.
23. German Catholic.
24. Gas Works.

STROBRIDGE & CO. LITH. CIN. O.

BIRDS-
BETHLE

BROAD ST.

MAPLE

UNION

MARKET ST.

ST.

CHURCH ST.

NISKY HILL
CEMETERY

LEHIGH RIVER

POPLAR

ST.

LINDEN ST.

PINE

SPRUCE

ST.

COURT

PEPPER

MECHANIC ST.

ELM

ST.

NEW

ST.

FIFTH

ST.

VINE

ST.

DRAWN BY O.H.BAILEY.

OF THE

MS, PA.

43

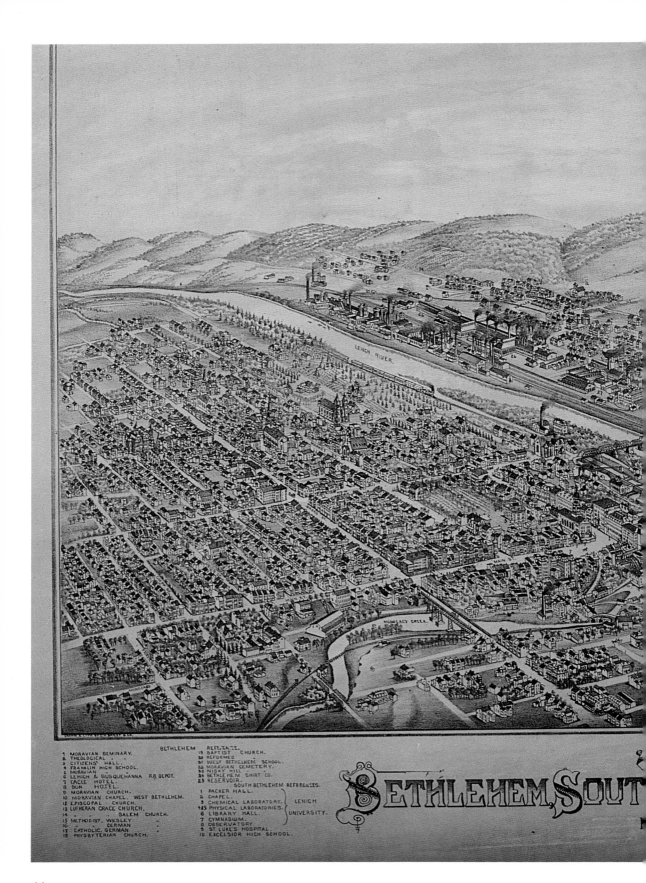

BETHLEHEM REFERENCES.
1 MORAVIAN SEMINARY.
2 THEOLOGICAL
3 CITIZENS' HALL.
4 FRANKLIN HIGH SCHOOL.
5 MORAVIAN.
6 LEHIGH & SUSQUEHANNA R.R. DEPOT.
7 EAGLE HOTEL.
8 SUN HOTEL.
9 MORAVIAN CHURCH.
10 MORAVIAN CHAPEL, WEST BETHLEHEM.
12 EPISCOPAL CHURCH.
13 LUTHERAN GRACE CHURCH.
14 " "   SALEM CHURCH.
15 METHODIST, WESLEY "
16 " GERMAN "
17 CATHOLIC, GERMAN "
18 PRESBYTERIAN CHURCH.

19 BAPTIST CHURCH.
21 REFORMED
31 WEST BETHLEHEM SCHOOL.
32 MORAVIAN CEMETERY.
33 NISKY HILL
34 BETHLEHEM SHIRT CO.
25 RESERVOIR.
          SOUTH BETHLEHEM REFERENCES.
1 PACKER HALL.
2 CHAPEL.
3 CHEMICAL LABORATORY. } LEHIGH
4&5 PHYSICAL LABORATORIES. }
6 LIBRARY HALL. } UNIVERSITY.
7 GYMNASIUM.
8 OBSERVATORY.
9 ST. LUKE'S HOSPITAL.
10 EXCELSIOR HIGH SCHOOL.

BETHLEHEM, SOUT

44

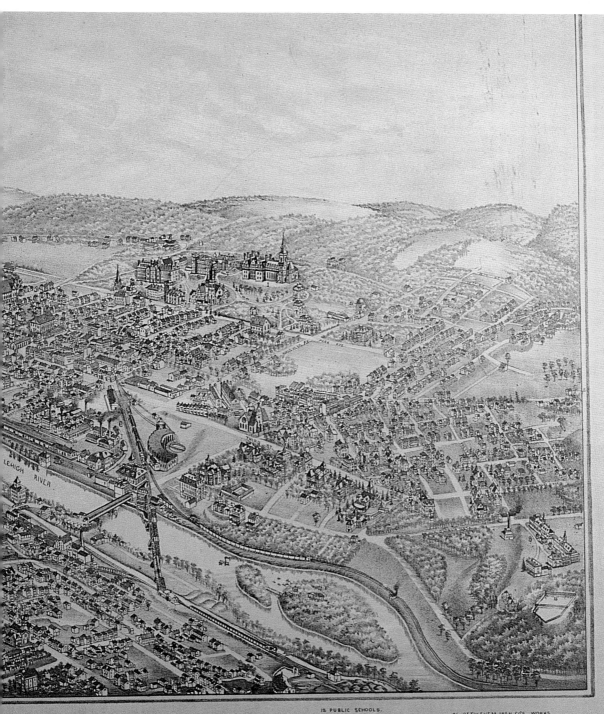

LEHIGH RIVER

WEST BETHLEHEM.

ANIA.
BOSTON.

12 PUBLIC SCHOOLS.
13 RESERVOIR.
14 R C CEMETERY.
15 CHURCH OF THE HOLY INFANCY." R. CATHOLIC.
16   "   - " NATIVITY, EPISCOPAL.
17 MORAVIAN   ) CHURCH
18 LUTHERAN-ST PETERS
19 FIRST PRESBYTERIAN
20 REFORMED
21 LEHIGH VALLEY HOUSE.
22 MANSION HOUSE.
23 EAGLE HOTEL.
24 MERCHANTS' HOTEL.
25 UNION DEPOT.

26 BETHLEHEM IRON CO'S WORKS.
27 LEHIGH ZINC & IRON CO'S "
28 LEHIGH VALLEY BOILER "
29 LEHIGH VALLEY BRASS   "
30 LEHIGH MANUFACTURING CO.
31 EXCELSIOR KNITTING MILL.
32 GAS WORKS.

45

DRAWN BY T.M.FOWLER, MORRISVILLE, PA

1. PUBLIC SCHOOLS.
2. SILK MILL.
3. PLANING MILL, SMITH & CLAWELL, PRO.
4. LUMBER, COAL & WOOD. DEALERS. BORHEK. & MIKSCH. PRO'PS.
5. FETTER HOUSE S.M.CRALL ....PRO.
6. BROADWAY HOUSE. ANTON. BOWMAN. "
7. ELECTRIC LIGHT PLANT.

WEST

LEHI

UNION ST.

NORTH ST.

FIRST AVE.

MONOCACY CREEK

FETTERS HOTEL

SPRING ST.

CONESTOGA ST.

WEST ST.

SECOND ST.

...WLER 1894.

PUBLISHED BY T.M. FOWLER & JAMES B. MOYER

THLEHEM,

PENNSYLVANIA.

4,

- CHURCHES -
A. MORAVIAN CHAPEL
B. TRINITY LUTHERAN CHURCH.
C. BETHANY REFORMED CHAPEL.

47

48

*Charles M. Schwab, 1862-1939, and Eugene G.
Grace, 1876-1960 (Bethlehem Steel, Frank O. Salis-
bury, artist).*

Twentieth-century Challenge and Response

In 1899 Bethlehem Steel Company was organized and obtained control of Bethlehem Iron Company. Bethlehem Steel Corporation was chartered on December 10, 1904 and Charles M. Schwab assumed the presidency. He had long been one of Andrew Carnegie's lieutenants and was the first president of United States Steel Corporation, from which office he had resigned in April 1903.

The early success of Bethlehem Steel was due, without question, to the genius of Charles M. Schwab.

Already an employee at the Bethlehem plant when Schwab acquired the company, Eugene G. Grace was working in the open hearth department. Recognizing Grace's abilities, Schwab selected Grace to be in charge of the erection of a new type of mill to make structural steel — a universal mill that could roll wide-flange shapes of far greater strength and less weight than those rolled on standard mills. The inventor, Henry Gray, offered it to Schwab who was quick to accept it. Schwab got his mill in 1908 and Grace ran it. America's major cities are monuments to the vision and determination of these men. Grace became president in 1916 and Schwab remained chairman of the board until his death in 1939.

In 1914, the outbreak of the first World War brought orders for military material. Bethlehem Steel's ability to turn it out in large quantities contributed greatly to the Allied cause.

As the war raged in Europe, public opinion in Bethlehem began to shift for the first time toward the consolidation of the Boroughs of Bethlehem and South Bethlehem. Charles M. Schwab and other Bethlehem Steel executives urged unification. In July 1917, voters of both boroughs cast their ballots for a single Bethlehem.

During the 1920's Bethlehem acquired additional steelmaking facilities. By 1939, Bethlehem had the ability to turn out steel products on a far greater scale than that called for in the first World War. After Pearl Harbor, all of Bethlehem's operations shifted to a war production basis.

Since its early days, the Bethlehem Plant has been a center for the development and production of special analysis steels. More manufactured steel products are made at Bethlehem than at any other plant in the country.

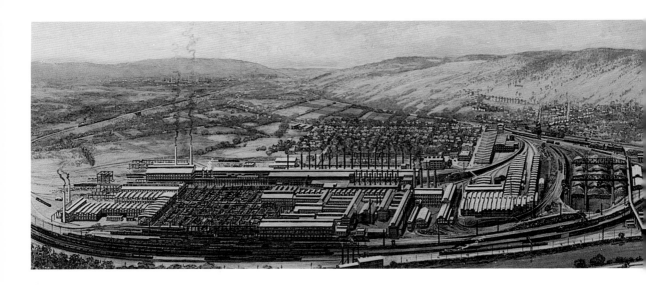

Bethlehem Steel Company, Reddington, Pa., Redding-ton Plant, 1916 (Bethlehem Steel, Edward W. Spofford, New York, delineator).

Bethlehem Steel Company, South Bethlehem, Pa.,
Bethlehem Plant, 1916 (Bethlehem Steel, Edward
W. Spofford, New York, delineator).

#1670A

Number Two Machine Shop, 1920. Built under the direction of John Fritz between 1887 and 1891. Almost one-quarter mile in length, it served for many years as the center of Bethlehem Steel Company's gun production (Bethlehem Steel Corporation Collection, Hugh Moore Historical Park and Museums Inc., Easton, Pennsylvania).

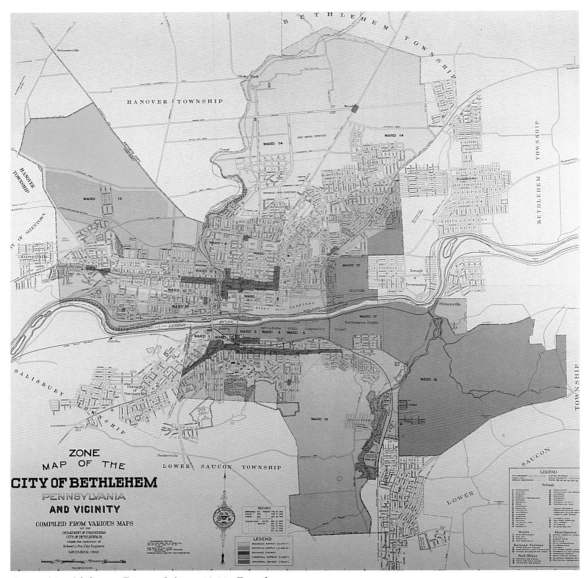

City of Bethlehem, Zoning Map, 1941. Population 58,490 in 1940. A community at the threshold of World War II (City of Bethlehem).

Bethlehem from the air, 1959. Population 75,409 in the 1960 census. Preparing for urban renewal and other municipal improvements (Bethlehem Steel).

Bethlehem from the air, 1969. Population 72,686 in the 1970 census. After a decade of civic development (Bethlehem Steel).

58

Approaching the Twenty-first Century

Bethlehem from the air, 1989. Population 71,428 in the 1990 census. Expansion continues in all geographic directions (City of Bethlehem).

Cultural Resources

1. Bethlehem Visitors Reception and Interpretation Center
   a. Upper Entrance - 509 Main Street
   b. Lower Entrance (future) — Old York Road

2. Kemerer Museum of Decorative Arts

3. Moravian Museum
   a. Gemeinhaus (1741)
   b. Apothecary Museum
   c. Nain Indian House

4. Moravian College Church Street Campus Priscilla Payne Hurd Center for Music and Art
   a. Single Brethren's House
   b. Payne Art Gallery

5. Historic Bethlehem Eighteenth-century Industrial Quarter
   a. Waterworks (1762)
   b. Springhouse
   c. Tannery (1761)
   d. Luckenbach Mill (1869)
   e. John Sebastian Goundie House (1810)

6. Burnside Plantation
   a. James Burnside House (1749, 1818)
   b. Barn (1841)
   c. Wagon Shed Interpretation Center

7. Moravian Archives

8. Sun Inn
   a. Inn (1758)
   b. Education and Tour Center
   c. Stable (future)

60

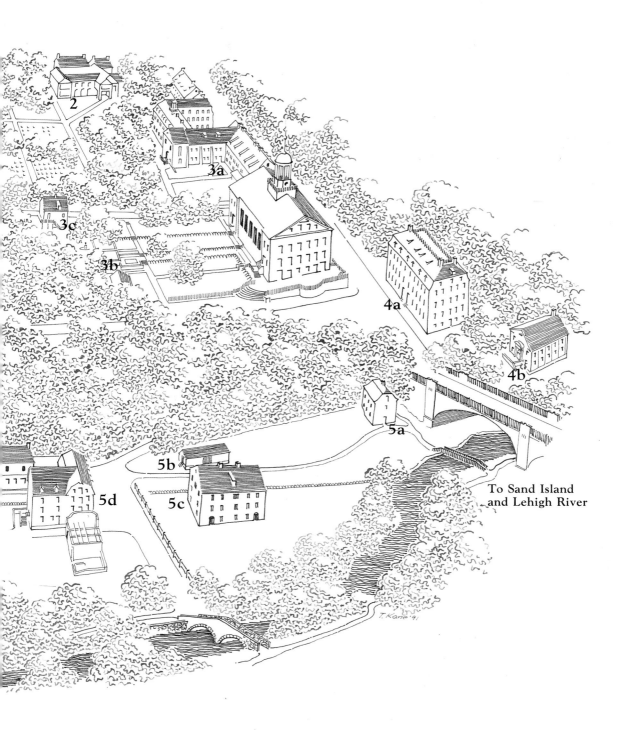

2

3a

3c

3b

4a

4b

5a

5b

5c

5d

To Sand Island
and Lehigh River

T. Kane '91

The Moravian community walking tour includes visits to 1803-06 Central Church, the 1741 Gemeinhaus, the 1751 Old Chapel and views Bell House square, God's Acre, the Sisters' House, the Widow's House, and the Brethren's House (Lee Butz, 1991).

Moravian Museum is located in the Gemeinhaus, Bethlehem's oldest building. The western and central sections were completed and occupied during the first year, 1741, and the eastern section was completed in 1742-3. Museum collections including early Moravian furniture, clocks, silver, musical instruments, religious articles and Seminary art and needlework, are presented and interpreted in period rooms and galleries.

The Gemeinhaus, one of the largest log buildings remaining in the United States, was designated a National Historic Landmark by the National Park Service in 1975 (Hub Willson, 1991).

On the first floor of the Gemeinhaus, the office of the administrator of Moravian properties is restored to its appearance during the last quarter of the eighteenth-century when it was occupied by John Christian A. de Schweinitz (Hub Willson, 1991).

*Kemerer Museum of Decorative Arts, looking north-
west (Lee Butz, 1991).*

The Kemerer Museum of Decorative Arts preserves and develops its core collections of American period furniture, regional paintings, glass, silver, ceramics, textiles, toys, prints, books, and related collectibles. Its galleries provide insight into the history of the Lehigh Valley in the eighteenth, nineteenth, and twentieth centuries through the interpretation of the decorative and folk arts.

Approaching Kemerer Museum of Decorative Arts from God's Acre (Ralph Schwarz, 1991).

Kemerer Museum of Decorative Arts at Christmas (Hub Willson, 1990).

The Eighteenth-century Industrial Quarter, looking south (Lee Butz, 1991).

Historic Bethlehem's Eighteenth-century Industrial Quarter, a ten-acre site, includes five restored buildings. Visitors can see the 1761 Tannery, the 1762 Waterworks, the 1869 Luckenbach Mill, the springhouse, and the 1810 residence of brewer John Sebastian Goundie. Other sites and buildings are under study for future restoration.

The restored John Sebastian Goundie House, 1810 (Ralph Schwarz, 1991).

Visitors tour the 1761 Tannery and the 1869 Luckenbach Mill (Hub Willson, 1991).

The restored Sun Inn (Lee Butz, 1991).

The Sun Inn, erected between 1758-1760, earned an enviable reputation, recounted by many distinguished visitors, for fine cuisine and excellent accommodations. Restored to its eighteenth-century appearance, it once again offers fine food together with tours of restored rooms.

East facade of the Sun Inn as seen from the stable yard (Ralph Schwarz, 1983).

The Sun Inn at Christmas (Hub Willson, 1990).

Burnside Plantation under restoration (Lee Butz, 1991).

Burnside Plantation, 1748-1848, a living history museum, linking the past with the present along the Monocacy Conservation Corridor, interprets the emergence and development of Moravian agricultural practice beginning with the residency of James Burnside.

Restored apparatus, illustrating horsepower technology in use after the bank barn was built in 1841 (Leonard Dimmick, 1991).

Wagon shed and corn crib with orchard at right (Ralph Schwarz, 1989).

Treasures from the collections of the Moravian
Archives, Bethlehem.

The Nativity (MAB, John Valentine Haidt).

*Christ after the Resurrection, exhibited at Moravian
Museum (MAB, John Valentine Haidt).*

*Rare Haidt watchcase, 1735.
John Valentine Haidt, 1700-
1780, goldsmith in London after
1724. Joined Moravians 1740,
came to Bethlehem 1754 as
preacher and painter, one of first
colonial Americans to treat religious subjects (MAB).*

Treasures from the collections of the Moravian
Historical Society, Nazareth.

*Violin made by John Antes, 1758, in Bethlehem. One of the first violins
made in America (MHS).*

*Four-stop organ made by David Tannenberg, 1776,
for the Chapel of the Single Brethren's House, Bethlehem (MHS).*

*Tile stove made by Joseph Huebener, before 1775,
in Lititz. Similar to those in use in Bethlehem (MHS).*

Moravian College, a coeducational liberal arts college that traces its origins to 1742.

Moravian College, Church Street Campus, Hurd Center for Music and Art, including the Payne Art Gallery and the Foy Concert Hall (Lee Butz, 1991).

pp. 76-77 Moravian College, Main Campus (Lee Butz, 1991).

Single Brethren's House, 1748, now part of Hurd Center for Music and Art (Ralph Schwarz, 1991).

Lehigh University, founded 1865, is located on three campuses comprising 1600 acres.

pp. 78-79. *Lehigh University, original Asa Packer Campus, (Lee Butz, 1991).*

Lehigh University, Master Plan, 1990. Murray H. Goodman Campus at bottom, Mountaintop Campus at center, Asa Packer Campus at top (Lehigh University).

Lehigh University, Mountaintop Campus. Iacocca Hall is the highest building in the Lehigh Valley (Bethlehem Steel).

Packer Memorial Church, Lehigh University, Asa Packer Campus. Scene of annual Bach Festival since 1912 (Hub Willson, 1991).

The Bach Choir of Bethlehem, Greg Funfgeld, Music Director and Conductor. Annual festivals initiated at Central Moravian Church, March 27, 1900, by the first American performance of the "Mass in B Minor" of Johann Sebastian Bach (H. Scott Heist, 1988).

South Bethlehem Historical Society preserves the rich heritage of the south side. Tours of churches and historic sites as well as lectures are held periodically (Hub Willson, 1991).

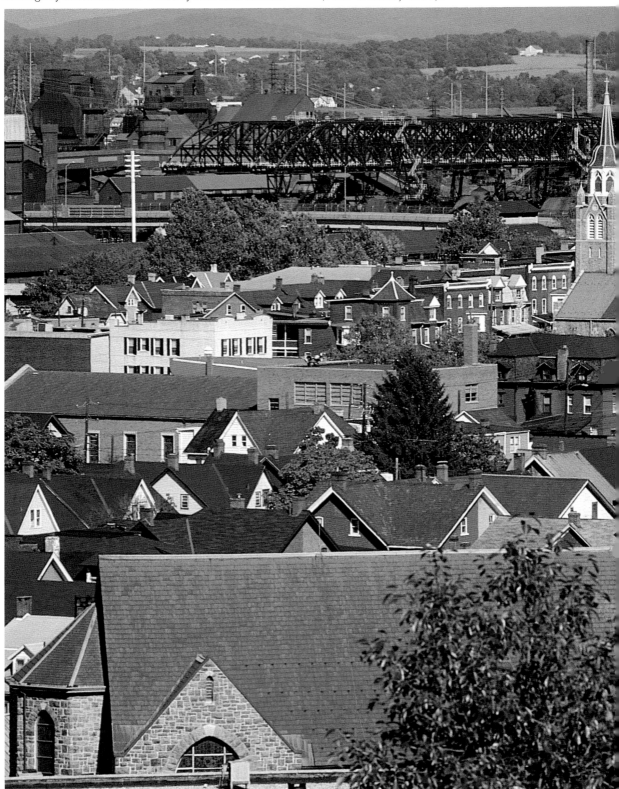

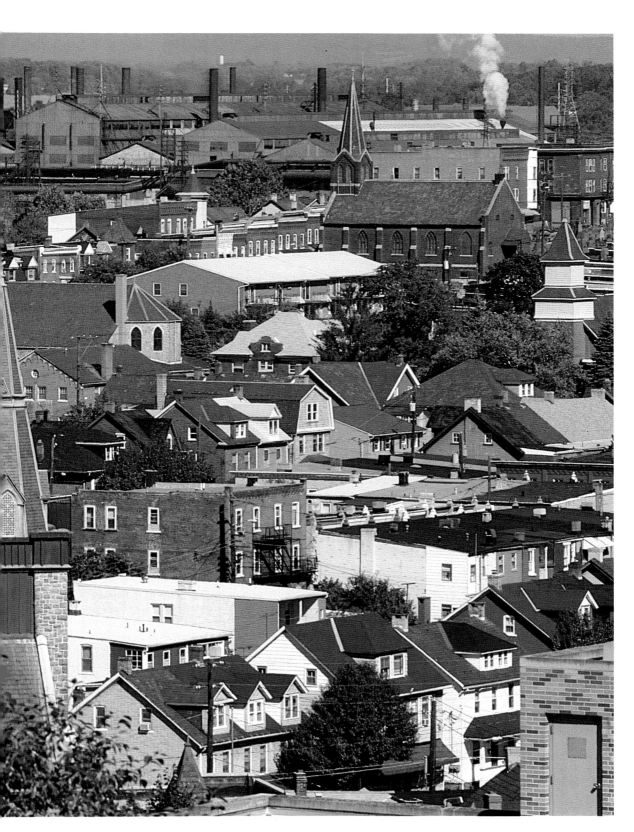

Blast furnaces seen from Nisky Hill, symbols of a great iron making tradition at the Bethlehem Plant (Bethlehem Steel).

Martin Tower, corporate headquarters of Bethlehem Steel Corporation and Union Pacific Corporation. Dun & Bradstreet also occupies space (Hub Willson, 1991).

"Little Man, What Now?," prophetic theme of a large canvas embroidery capturing the vibrations and mystery behind a landscape of steel (Allentown Art Museum, Mildred T. Johnstone, 1949).

Molten iron is poured into one of two basic oxygen
furnace vessels at Bethlehem Steel Corporation's Structural Products Division in Bethlehem, where it is re-
fined into steel (Bethlehem Steel, 1990).

Lehigh Valley Industrial Park, 236 industries creating
over 10,000 jobs (LVIP, 1990).

Allentown-Bethlehem-Easton International Airport
terminal (Hub Willson, 1991).

Shopping on Main Street (Hub Willson, 1991).

Entertainment on Fourth Street (Hub Willson, 1991).

Musikfest '91 (Hub Willson, 1991).

Celtic Classic '90, annual Highland games and festival (Hub Willson, 1990).

Celtic Classic '90 (Hub Willson, 1990).

Musikfest tents at Volksplatz, annual event presenting musical performances of a wide variety for the enjoyment of the general public (Hub Willson, 1989).

The City Center. Bethlehem Public Library, Town Hall and government offices (Lee Butz, 1991).

The City Center Plaza, Blumenplatz star of Bethlehem (Ralph Schwarz, 1991).

Sand Island, enhanced active and passive recreational facilities for public use and enjoyment (Lee Butz, 1991).

Bicycling along the Lehigh Canal, part of National Heritage Corridor (Hub Willson, 1991).

Christmas at the City Center on historic Church Street (Hub Willson, 1990).

December lantern walking tours (Hub Willson, 1990).

95

1762 Waterworks in winter. Earliest technology for municipal water distribution in America. It was desig-nated a National Historic Landmark by the National Park Service in 1981 (Hub Willson, 1990).